THIS PLANNER
Belongs To:

LIFE *Assessment*

SUMMARIZE HOW YOU **FEEL** ABOUT YOUR LIFE

TOP 3 AREAS OF YOUR LIFE YOU'D LIKE TO **IMPROVE**

01

02

03

3 WAYS YOU CAN **ACCOMPLISH** YOUR LIFE GOALS

SELF CARE *Planner*

Self-care involves taking care of yourself emotionally, mentally and physically.
Create a self-care plan by adding activities to the categories below.

MENTAL SELF-CARE

PHYSICAL SELF-CARE (GET ACTIVE)

EMOTIONAL SELF-CARE

DAILY HABITS (SLEEP, ETC.)

REACH OUT (SOCIALIZE)

SUPPORT NETWORK

OTHER:

SELF CARE *Focus*

TOP 3 SELF-CARE ACTIVITIES   HOW THEY MAKE ME FEEL

OTHER SELF-CARE ACTIVITIES THAT MAKE ME HAPPY

01

02

03

FAVORITE QUOTES/WORDS OF ENCOURAGEMENT

DEAR FUTURE *Self*...

FOCUS ON YOUR VISION OF A HAPPY FUTURE

FAMILY GOALS	CAREER GOALS

SELF CARE	RELATIONSHIP

HEALTH GOALS	FRIENDSHIPS

PERSONAL	FINANCIAL

TRAVEL	PASSIONS

NEW SKILLS	OTHER

5 YEARS FROM NOW	10 YEARS FROM NOW

ANXIETY Tracker

Document the days when you experienced anxiety. This page includes a 3-week tracker.

ANXIETY LEVELS (1-MILD, 10 SEVERE)

MON	01	02	03	04	05	06	07	08	09	10	11	12
TUE	01	02	03	04	05	06	07	08	09	10	11	12
WED	01	02	03	04	05	06	07	08	09	10	11	12
THU	01	02	03	04	05	06	07	08	09	10	11	12
FRI	01	02	03	04	05	06	07	08	09	10	11	12
SAT	01	02	03	04	05	06	07	08	09	10	11	12
SUN	01	02	03	04	05	06	07	08	09	10	11	12
MON	01	02	03	04	05	06	07	08	09	10	11	12
TUE	01	02	03	04	05	06	07	08	09	10	11	12
WED	01	02	03	04	05	06	07	08	09	10	11	12
THU	01	02	03	04	05	06	07	08	09	10	11	12
FRI	01	02	03	04	05	06	07	08	09	10	11	12
SAT	01	02	03	04	05	06	07	08	09	10	11	12
SUN	01	02	03	04	05	06	07	08	09	10	11	12
MON	01	02	03	04	05	06	07	08	09	10	11	12
TUE	01	02	03	04	05	06	07	08	09	10	11	12
WED	01	02	03	04	05	06	07	08	09	10	11	12
THU	01	02	03	04	05	06	07	08	09	10	11	12
FRI	01	02	03	04	05	06	07	08	09	10	11	12
SAT	01	02	03	04	05	06	07	08	09	10	11	12
SUN	01	02	03	04	05	06	07	08	09	10	11	12

NOTES:

DATE I STARTED TRACKING:

ANXIETY Tracker

Document the days when you experienced anxiety. This page includes a 3-week tracker.

ANXIETY LEVELS (1-MILD, 10 SEVERE)

Day													NOTES:
MON	01	02	03	04	05	06	07	08	09	10	11	12	
TUE	01	02	03	04	05	06	07	08	09	10	11	12	
WED	01	02	03	04	05	06	07	08	09	10	11	12	
THU	01	02	03	04	05	06	07	08	09	10	11	12	
FRI	01	02	03	04	05	06	07	08	09	10	11	12	
SAT	01	02	03	04	05	06	07	08	09	10	11	12	
SUN	01	02	03	04	05	06	07	08	09	10	11	12	
MON	01	02	03	04	05	06	07	08	09	10	11	12	
TUE	01	02	03	04	05	06	07	08	09	10	11	12	
WED	01	02	03	04	05	06	07	08	09	10	11	12	
THU	01	02	03	04	05	06	07	08	09	10	11	12	
FRI	01	02	03	04	05	06	07	08	09	10	11	12	
SAT	01	02	03	04	05	06	07	08	09	10	11	12	
SUN	01	02	03	04	05	06	07	08	09	10	11	12	
MON	01	02	03	04	05	06	07	08	09	10	11	12	
TUE	01	02	03	04	05	06	07	08	09	10	11	12	
WED	01	02	03	04	05	06	07	08	09	10	11	12	
THU	01	02	03	04	05	06	07	08	09	10	11	12	
FRI	01	02	03	04	05	06	07	08	09	10	11	12	
SAT	01	02	03	04	05	06	07	08	09	10	11	12	
SUN	01	02	03	04	05	06	07	08	09	10	11	12	

DATE I STARTED TRACKING:

ANXIETY Tracker

Document the days when you experienced anxiety. This page includes a 3-week tracker.

ANXIETY LEVELS (1-MILD, 10 SEVERE)

MON	01	02	03	04	05	06	07	08	09	10	11	12
TUE	01	02	03	04	05	06	07	08	09	10	11	12
WED	01	02	03	04	05	06	07	08	09	10	11	12
THU	01	02	03	04	05	06	07	08	09	10	11	12
FRI	01	02	03	04	05	06	07	08	09	10	11	12
SAT	01	02	03	04	05	06	07	08	09	10	11	12
SUN	01	02	03	04	05	06	07	08	09	10	11	12
MON	01	02	03	04	05	06	07	08	09	10	11	12
TUE	01	02	03	04	05	06	07	08	09	10	11	12
WED	01	02	03	04	05	06	07	08	09	10	11	12
THU	01	02	03	04	05	06	07	08	09	10	11	12
FRI	01	02	03	04	05	06	07	08	09	10	11	12
SAT	01	02	03	04	05	06	07	08	09	10	11	12
SUN	01	02	03	04	05	06	07	08	09	10	11	12
MON	01	02	03	04	05	06	07	08	09	10	11	12
TUE	01	02	03	04	05	06	07	08	09	10	11	12
WED	01	02	03	04	05	06	07	08	09	10	11	12
THU	01	02	03	04	05	06	07	08	09	10	11	12
FRI	01	02	03	04	05	06	07	08	09	10	11	12
SAT	01	02	03	04	05	06	07	08	09	10	11	12
SUN	01	02	03	04	05	06	07	08	09	10	11	12

NOTES:

DATE I STARTED TRACKING:

ANXIETY *Tracker*

Document the days when you experienced anxiety. This page includes a 3-week tracker.

ANXIETY LEVELS (1-MILD, 10 SEVERE)

Day													NOTES:
MON	01	02	03	04	05	06	07	08	09	10	11	12	
TUE	01	02	03	04	05	06	07	08	09	10	11	12	
WED	01	02	03	04	05	06	07	08	09	10	11	12	
THU	01	02	03	04	05	06	07	08	09	10	11	12	
FRI	01	02	03	04	05	06	07	08	09	10	11	12	
SAT	01	02	03	04	05	06	07	08	09	10	11	12	
SUN	01	02	03	04	05	06	07	08	09	10	11	12	
MON	01	02	03	04	05	06	07	08	09	10	11	12	
TUE	01	02	03	04	05	06	07	08	09	10	11	12	
WED	01	02	03	04	05	06	07	08	09	10	11	12	
THU	01	02	03	04	05	06	07	08	09	10	11	12	
FRI	01	02	03	04	05	06	07	08	09	10	11	12	
SAT	01	02	03	04	05	06	07	08	09	10	11	12	
SUN	01	02	03	04	05	06	07	08	09	10	11	12	
MON	01	02	03	04	05	06	07	08	09	10	11	12	
TUE	01	02	03	04	05	06	07	08	09	10	11	12	
WED	01	02	03	04	05	06	07	08	09	10	11	12	
THU	01	02	03	04	05	06	07	08	09	10	11	12	
FRI	01	02	03	04	05	06	07	08	09	10	11	12	
SAT	01	02	03	04	05	06	07	08	09	10	11	12	
SUN	01	02	03	04	05	06	07	08	09	10	11	12	

DATE I STARTED TRACKING:

HAPPINESS Is...

Complete the following sentences to refocus your mind on the joys in your life:

I FEEL MOST RELAXED WHEN:

I AM LESS STRESSED WHEN:

MY STRENGTHS ARE:

I AM A GOOD FRIEND BECAUSE:

I AM MOST EXCITED BY:

I AM MOST FOCUSED WHEN:

I FEEL MOST APPRECIATED WHEN:

I AM MOST MOTIVATED WHEN:

HAPPINESS Tracker

Keep track of how often you feel happy and calm and what you did to minimize negative responses.

DATE:

DATE:

HAPPINESS RATING: ☆☆☆☆☆

HAPPINESS RATING: ☆☆☆☆☆

DATE:

DATE:

HAPPINESS RATING: ☆☆☆☆☆

HAPPINESS RATING: ☆☆☆☆☆

DATE:

DATE:

HAPPINESS RATING: ☆☆☆☆☆

HAPPINESS RATING: ☆☆☆☆☆

HAPPINESS Tracker

Keep track of how often you feel happy and calm and what you did to minimize negative responses.

DATE:

DATE:

HAPPINESS RATING: ☆☆☆☆☆

HAPPINESS RATING: ☆☆☆☆☆

DATE:

DATE:

HAPPINESS RATING: ☆☆☆☆☆

HAPPINESS RATING: ☆☆☆☆☆

DATE:

DATE:

HAPPINESS RATING:

HAPPINESS RATING:

HAPPINESS *Tracker*

Keep track of how often you feel happy and calm and what you did to minimize negative responses.

DATE:

DATE:

HAPPINESS RATING: ☆☆☆☆☆

HAPPINESS RATING: ☆☆☆☆☆

DATE:

DATE:

HAPPINESS RATING: ☆☆☆☆☆

HAPPINESS RATING: ☆☆☆☆☆

DATE:

DATE:

HAPPINESS RATING: ☆☆☆☆☆

HAPPINESS RATING: ☆☆☆☆☆

HAPPINESS Tracker

Keep track of how often you feel happy and calm and what you did to minimize negative responses.

DATE:

DATE:

HAPPINESS RATING: ☆☆☆☆☆

HAPPINESS RATING: ☆☆☆☆☆

DATE:

DATE:

HAPPINESS RATING: ☆☆☆☆☆

HAPPINESS RATING: ☆☆☆☆☆

DATE:

DATE:

HAPPINESS RATING:

HAPPINESS RATING:

TRIGGER Tracker

Keep track of experiences that generate negative thoughts and emotions.

DATE	INCIDENT	REACTION

TRIGGER Tracker

Keep track of experiences that generate negative thoughts and emotions.

DATE	INCIDENT	REACTION

TRIGGER *Tracker*

Keep track of experiences that generate negative thoughts and emotions.

DATE	INCIDENT	REACTION

GRATEFUL *Heart*

DATE   WHAT I AM GRATEFUL FOR

GRATEFUL *Heart*

DATE　　　　　　　　　　WHAT I AM GRATEFUL FOR

GRATEFUL *Heart*

DATE — WHAT I AM GRATEFUL FOR

MOOD *Chart*

Use the wheel below to document your moods every month.
Use 3 different colors to represent positive, negative or neutral emotions.

☐ POSITIVE ☐ NEGATIVE ☐ NEUTRAL

MONTH:

SLEEP *Tracker*

MONTH:

Sleep plays a major factor in our ability to cope with anxiety. Keep track of your sleep pattern in order to determine how the amount of rest may be affecting your mental health.

DAY	HOURS SLEPT	QUALITY OF SLEEP	THOUGHTS
1			
2			
3			
4			
5			
6			
7			
8			
9			
10			
11			
12			
13			
14			
15			
16			
17			
18			
19			
20			
21			
22			
23			
24			
25			
26			
27			
28			
29			
30			
31			

DATE:

DAILY *Reflection*

HOW I FEEL TODAY   **MY GREATEST CHALLENGE**

MOOD TRACKER:

MORNING: **EVENING:**

I FELT HAPPY WHEN: **I FELT EXCITED WHEN:**   **I FELT ENERGIZED WHEN:**

Today's Highlights

What I'm Grateful For Today

DATE:

DAILY *Reflection*

HOW I FEEL TODAY **MY GREATEST CHALLENGE**

MOOD TRACKER:

MORNING: EVENING:

I FELT HAPPY WHEN: I FELT EXCITED WHEN: I FELT ENERGIZED WHEN:

Today's Highlights

What I'm Grateful For Today

DATE:

DAILY *Reflection*

HOW I FEEL TODAY **MY GREATEST CHALLENGE**

MOOD TRACKER:

MORNING: EVENING:

I FELT HAPPY WHEN: I FELT EXCITED WHEN: I FELT ENERGIZED WHEN:

Today's Highlights

What I'm Grateful For Today

DATE:

DAILY Reflection

HOW I FEEL TODAY **MY GREATEST CHALLENGE**

MOOD TRACKER:

MORNING: **EVENING:**

I FELT HAPPY WHEN: **I FELT EXCITED WHEN:** **I FELT ENERGIZED WHEN:**

Today's Highlights

What I'm Grateful For Today

DATE:

DAILY *Reflection*

HOW I FEEL TODAY **MY GREATEST CHALLENGE**

MOOD TRACKER:

MORNING: EVENING:

I FELT HAPPY WHEN: I FELT EXCITED WHEN: I FELT ENERGIZED WHEN:

Today's Highlights

What I'm Grateful For Today

DATE:

DAILY *Reflection*

HOW I FEEL TODAY

MY GREATEST CHALLENGE

MOOD TRACKER:

MORNING:

EVENING:

I FELT HAPPY WHEN:

I FELT EXCITED WHEN:

I FELT ENERGIZED WHEN:

Today's Highlights

What I'm Grateful For Today

DATE:

DAILY *Reflection*

HOW I FEEL TODAY　　　　　　　　　　　　　　　**MY GREATEST CHALLENGE**

MOOD TRACKER:

MORNING:　　　　　　　　　　EVENING:

I FELT HAPPY WHEN:　　　　**I FELT EXCITED WHEN:**　　　　**I FELT ENERGIZED WHEN:**

Today's Highlights

What I'm Grateful For Today

WEEKLY Assessment

	SLEEP	MOOD	POSITIVES	NEGATIVES
MONDAY				
TUESDAY				
WEDNESDAY				
THURSDAY				
FRIDAY				
SATURADY				
SUNDAY				

DATE:

DAILY *Reflection*

HOW I FEEL TODAY **MY GREATEST CHALLENGE**

MOOD TRACKER:

MORNING: **EVENING:**

I FELT HAPPY WHEN: **I FELT EXCITED WHEN:** **I FELT ENERGIZED WHEN:**

Today's Highlights

What I'm Grateful For Today

DATE:

DAILY Reflection

HOW I FEEL TODAY **MY GREATEST CHALLENGE**

MOOD TRACKER:

MORNING: EVENING:

I FELT HAPPY WHEN: **I FELT EXCITED WHEN:** **I FELT ENERGIZED WHEN:**

Today's Highlights

What I'm Grateful For Today

DATE:

DAILY Reflection

HOW I FEEL TODAY   **MY GREATEST CHALLENGE**

MOOD TRACKER:

MORNING: EVENING:

I FELT HAPPY WHEN: **I FELT EXCITED WHEN:**   **I FELT ENERGIZED WHEN:**

Today's Highlights

What I'm Grateful For Today

DATE:

DAILY Reflection

HOW I FEEL TODAY

MY GREATEST CHALLENGE

MOOD TRACKER:

MORNING:

EVENING:

I FELT HAPPY WHEN:

I FELT EXCITED WHEN:

I FELT ENERGIZED WHEN:

Today's Highlights

What I'm Grateful For Today

DATE:

DAILY Reflection

HOW I FEEL TODAY MY GREATEST CHALLENGE

MOOD TRACKER:

MORNING: EVENING:

I FELT HAPPY WHEN: I FELT EXCITED WHEN: I FELT ENERGIZED WHEN:

Today's Highlights

What I'm Grateful For Today

DAILY *Reflection*

DATE:

HOW I FEEL TODAY

MY GREATEST CHALLENGE

MOOD TRACKER:

MORNING:

EVENING:

I FELT HAPPY WHEN:

I FELT EXCITED WHEN:

I FELT ENERGIZED WHEN:

Today's Highlights

What I'm Grateful For Today

DATE:

DAILY Reflection

HOW I FEEL TODAY MY GREATEST CHALLENGE

MOOD TRACKER:

MORNING: EVENING:

I FELT HAPPY WHEN: I FELT EXCITED WHEN: I FELT ENERGIZED WHEN:

Today's Highlights

What I'm Grateful For Today

WEEKLY Assessment

	SLEEP	MOOD	POSITIVES	NEGATIVES
MONDAY				
TUESDAY				
WEDNESDAY				
THURSDAY				
FRIDAY				
SATURDAY				
SUNDAY				

DATE:

DAILY *Reflection*

HOW I FEEL TODAY   **MY GREATEST CHALLENGE**

MOOD TRACKER:

MORNING: EVENING:

I FELT HAPPY WHEN: I FELT EXCITED WHEN: I FELT ENERGIZED WHEN:

Today's Highlights

What I'm Grateful For Today

DATE:

DAILY *Reflection*

HOW I FEEL TODAY **MY GREATEST CHALLENGE**

MOOD TRACKER:

MORNING: **EVENING:**

I FELT HAPPY WHEN: **I FELT EXCITED WHEN:** **I FELT ENERGIZED WHEN:**

Today's Highlights

What I'm Grateful For Today

DATE:

DAILY Reflection

HOW I FEEL TODAY **MY GREATEST CHALLENGE**

MOOD TRACKER:

MORNING: **EVENING:**

I FELT HAPPY WHEN: **I FELT EXCITED WHEN:** **I FELT ENERGIZED WHEN:**

Today's Highlights

What I'm Grateful For Today

DATE:

DAILY *Reflection*

HOW I FEEL TODAY **MY GREATEST CHALLENGE**

MOOD TRACKER:

MORNING: EVENING:

I FELT HAPPY WHEN: **I FELT EXCITED WHEN:** **I FELT ENERGIZED WHEN:**

Today's Highlights

What I'm Grateful For Today

DATE:

DAILY *Reflection*

HOW I FEEL TODAY **MY GREATEST CHALLENGE**

MOOD TRACKER:

MORNING: EVENING:

I FELT HAPPY WHEN: I FELT EXCITED WHEN: I FELT ENERGIZED WHEN:

Today's Highlights

What I'm Grateful For Today

DATE:

DAILY *Reflection*

HOW I FEEL TODAY

MY GREATEST CHALLENGE

MOOD TRACKER:

MORNING:

EVENING:

I FELT HAPPY WHEN:

I FELT EXCITED WHEN:

I FELT ENERGIZED WHEN:

Today's Highlights

What I'm Grateful For Today

DATE:

DAILY *Reflection*

HOW I FEEL TODAY **MY GREATEST CHALLENGE**

MOOD TRACKER:

MORNING: EVENING:

I FELT HAPPY WHEN: **I FELT EXCITED WHEN:** **I FELT ENERGIZED WHEN:**

Today's Highlights

What I'm Grateful For Today

WEEKLY Assessment

	SLEEP	MOOD	POSITIVES	NEGATIVES
MONDAY				
TUESDAY				
WEDNESDAY				
THURSDAY				
FRIDAY				
SATURADY				
SUNDAY				

DATE:

DAILY *Reflection*

HOW I FEEL TODAY MY GREATEST CHALLENGE

MOOD TRACKER:

MORNING: EVENING:

I FELT HAPPY WHEN: I FELT EXCITED WHEN: I FELT ENERGIZED WHEN:

Today's Highlights

What I'm Grateful For Today

DATE:

DAILY *Reflection*

HOW I FEEL TODAY   **MY GREATEST CHALLENGE**

MOOD TRACKER:

MORNING: EVENING:

I FELT HAPPY WHEN: I FELT EXCITED WHEN: I FELT ENERGIZED WHEN:

Today's Highlights

What I'm Grateful For Today

DATE:

DAILY Reflection

HOW I FEEL TODAY   **MY GREATEST CHALLENGE**

MOOD TRACKER:

MORNING: EVENING:

I FELT HAPPY WHEN: I FELT EXCITED WHEN: I FELT ENERGIZED WHEN:

Today's Highlights

What I'm Grateful For Today

DAILY *Reflection*

DATE:

HOW I FEEL TODAY

MY GREATEST CHALLENGE

MOOD TRACKER:

MORNING:

EVENING:

I FELT HAPPY WHEN:

I FELT EXCITED WHEN:

I FELT ENERGIZED WHEN:

Today's Highlights

What I'm Grateful For Today

DATE:

DAILY Reflection

HOW I FEEL TODAY **MY GREATEST CHALLENGE**

MOOD TRACKER:

MORNING: EVENING:

I FELT HAPPY WHEN: I FELT EXCITED WHEN: I FELT ENERGIZED WHEN:

Today's Highlights

What I'm Grateful For Today

DATE:

DAILY *Reflection*

HOW I FEEL TODAY **MY GREATEST CHALLENGE**

MOOD TRACKER:

MORNING: **EVENING:**

I FELT HAPPY WHEN: **I FELT EXCITED WHEN:** **I FELT ENERGIZED WHEN:**

Today's Highlights

What I'm Grateful For Today

DATE:

DAILY *Reflection*

HOW I FEEL TODAY MY GREATEST CHALLENGE

MOOD TRACKER:

MORNING: EVENING:

I FELT HAPPY WHEN: I FELT EXCITED WHEN: I FELT ENERGIZED WHEN:

Today's Highlights

What I'm Grateful For Today

WEEKLY *Assessment*

	SLEEP	MOOD	POSITIVES	NEGATIVES
MONDAY				
TUESDAY				
WEDNESDAY				
THURSDAY				
FRIDAY				
SATURADY				
SUNDAY				

MOOD *Chart*

Use the wheel below to document your moods every month.
Use 3 different colors to represent positive, negative or neutral emotions.

☐ POSITIVE   ☐ NEGATIVE   ☐ NEUTRAL

MONTH:

SLEEP *Tracker*

MONTH:

Sleep plays a major factor in our ability to cope with anxiety. Keep track of your sleep pattern in order to determine how the amount of rest may be affecting your mental health.

DAY	HOURS SLEPT	QUALITY OF SLEEP	THOUGHTS
1			
2			
3			
4			
5			
6			
7			
8			
9			
10			
11			
12			
13			
14			
15			
16			
17			
18			
19			
20			
21			
22			
23			
24			
25			
26			
27			
28			
29			
30			
31			

DAILY *Reflection*

DATE:

HOW I FEEL TODAY

MY GREATEST CHALLENGE

MOOD TRACKER:

MORNING:

EVENING:

I FELT HAPPY WHEN:

I FELT EXCITED WHEN:

I FELT ENERGIZED WHEN:

Today's Highlights

What I'm Grateful For Today

DATE:

DAILY Reflection

HOW I FEEL TODAY

MY GREATEST CHALLENGE

MOOD TRACKER:

MORNING:

EVENING:

I FELT HAPPY WHEN:

I FELT EXCITED WHEN:

I FELT ENERGIZED WHEN:

Today's Highlights

What I'm Grateful For Today

DATE:

DAILY *Reflection*

HOW I FEEL TODAY MY GREATEST CHALLENGE

MOOD TRACKER:

MORNING: EVENING:

I FELT HAPPY WHEN: I FELT EXCITED WHEN: I FELT ENERGIZED WHEN:

Today's Highlights

What I'm Grateful For Today

DATE:

DAILY *Reflection*

HOW I FEEL TODAY   **MY GREATEST CHALLENGE**

MOOD TRACKER:

MORNING: EVENING:

I FELT HAPPY WHEN: **I FELT EXCITED WHEN:**   **I FELT ENERGIZED WHEN:**

Today's Highlights

What I'm Grateful For Today

DATE:

DAILY Reflection

HOW I FEEL TODAY   **MY GREATEST CHALLENGE**

MOOD TRACKER:

MORNING: **EVENING:**

I FELT HAPPY WHEN: **I FELT EXCITED WHEN:**   **I FELT ENERGIZED WHEN:**

Today's Highlights

What I'm Grateful For Today

DATE:

DAILY *Reflection*

HOW I FEEL TODAY

MY GREATEST CHALLENGE

MOOD TRACKER:

MORNING:

EVENING:

I FELT HAPPY WHEN:

I FELT EXCITED WHEN:

I FELT ENERGIZED WHEN:

Today's Highlights

What I'm Grateful For Today

DATE:

DAILY *Reflection*

HOW I FEEL TODAY MY GREATEST CHALLENGE

MOOD TRACKER:

MORNING: EVENING:

I FELT HAPPY WHEN: I FELT EXCITED WHEN: I FELT ENERGIZED WHEN:

Today's Highlights

What I'm Grateful For Today

WEEKLY Assessment

	SLEEP	MOOD	POSITIVES	NEGATIVES
MONDAY				
TUESDAY				
WEDNESDAY				
THURSDAY				
FRIDAY				
SATURADY				
SUNDAY				

DATE:

DAILY *Reflection*

HOW I FEEL TODAY   **MY GREATEST CHALLENGE**

MOOD TRACKER:

MORNING: EVENING:

I FELT HAPPY WHEN: **I FELT EXCITED WHEN:**   **I FELT ENERGIZED WHEN:**

Today's Highlights

What I'm Grateful For Today

DATE:

DAILY *Reflection*

HOW I FEEL TODAY   **MY GREATEST CHALLENGE**

MOOD TRACKER:

MORNING: EVENING:

I FELT HAPPY WHEN: **I FELT EXCITED WHEN:**   **I FELT ENERGIZED WHEN:**

Today's Highlights

What I'm Grateful For Today

DATE:

DAILY *Reflection*

HOW I FEEL TODAY **MY GREATEST CHALLENGE**

MOOD TRACKER:

MORNING: **EVENING:**

I FELT HAPPY WHEN: **I FELT EXCITED WHEN:** **I FELT ENERGIZED WHEN:**

Today's Highlights

What I'm Grateful For Today

DATE:

DAILY *Reflection*

HOW I FEEL TODAY   **MY GREATEST CHALLENGE**

MOOD TRACKER:

MORNING: EVENING:

I FELT HAPPY WHEN: **I FELT EXCITED WHEN:**   **I FELT ENERGIZED WHEN:**

Today's Highlights

What I'm Grateful For Today

DAILY *Reflection*

DATE:

HOW I FEEL TODAY

MY GREATEST CHALLENGE

MOOD TRACKER:

MORNING:

EVENING:

I FELT HAPPY WHEN:

I FELT EXCITED WHEN:

I FELT ENERGIZED WHEN:

Today's Highlights

What I'm Grateful For Today

DAILY *Reflection*

DATE:

HOW I FEEL TODAY

MY GREATEST CHALLENGE

MOOD TRACKER:

MORNING:

EVENING:

I FELT HAPPY WHEN:

I FELT EXCITED WHEN:

I FELT ENERGIZED WHEN:

Today's Highlights

What I'm Grateful For Today

DATE:

DAILY *Reflection*

HOW I FEEL TODAY **MY GREATEST CHALLENGE**

MOOD TRACKER:

MORNING: EVENING:

I FELT HAPPY WHEN: I FELT EXCITED WHEN: I FELT ENERGIZED WHEN:

Today's Highlights

What I'm Grateful For Today

WEEKLY *Assessment*

	SLEEP	MOOD	POSITIVES	NEGATIVES
MONDAY				
TUESDAY				
WEDNESDAY				
THURSDAY				
FRIDAY				
SATURADY				
SUNDAY				

DATE:

DAILY Reflection

HOW I FEEL TODAY MY GREATEST CHALLENGE

MOOD TRACKER:

MORNING: EVENING:

I FELT HAPPY WHEN: I FELT EXCITED WHEN: I FELT ENERGIZED WHEN:

Today's Highlights

What I'm Grateful For Today

DATE:

DAILY *Reflection*

HOW I FEEL TODAY **MY GREATEST CHALLENGE**

MOOD TRACKER:

MORNING: EVENING:

I FELT HAPPY WHEN: I FELT EXCITED WHEN: I FELT ENERGIZED WHEN:

Today's Highlights

What I'm Grateful For Today

DATE:

DAILY *Reflection*

HOW I FEEL TODAY **MY GREATEST CHALLENGE**

MOOD TRACKER:

MORNING: EVENING:

I FELT HAPPY WHEN: **I FELT EXCITED WHEN:** **I FELT ENERGIZED WHEN:**

Today's Highlights

What I'm Grateful For Today

DATE:

DAILY *Reflection*

HOW I FEEL TODAY MY GREATEST CHALLENGE

MOOD TRACKER:

MORNING: EVENING:

I FELT HAPPY WHEN: I FELT EXCITED WHEN: I FELT ENERGIZED WHEN:

Today's Highlights

What I'm Grateful For Today

DAILY *Reflection*

DATE:

HOW I FEEL TODAY

MY GREATEST CHALLENGE

MOOD TRACKER:

MORNING:

EVENING:

I FELT HAPPY WHEN:

I FELT EXCITED WHEN:

I FELT ENERGIZED WHEN:

Today's Highlights

What I'm Grateful For Today

DAILY Reflection

DATE:

HOW I FEEL TODAY

MY GREATEST CHALLENGE

MOOD TRACKER:

MORNING:

EVENING:

I FELT HAPPY WHEN:

I FELT EXCITED WHEN:

I FELT ENERGIZED WHEN:

Today's Highlights

What I'm Grateful For Today

DATE:

DAILY *Reflection*

HOW I FEEL TODAY **MY GREATEST CHALLENGE**

MOOD TRACKER:

MORNING: EVENING:

I FELT HAPPY WHEN: **I FELT EXCITED WHEN:** **I FELT ENERGIZED WHEN:**

Today's Highlights

What I'm Grateful For Today

WEEKLY Assessment

	SLEEP	MOOD	POSITIVES	NEGATIVES
MONDAY				
TUESDAY				
WEDNESDAY				
THURSDAY				
FRIDAY				
SATURADY				
SUNDAY				

DATE:

DAILY Reflection

HOW I FEEL TODAY

MY GREATEST CHALLENGE

MOOD TRACKER:

MORNING:

EVENING:

I FELT HAPPY WHEN:

I FELT EXCITED WHEN:

I FELT ENERGIZED WHEN:

Today's Highlights

What I'm Grateful For Today

DATE:

DAILY *Reflection*

HOW I FEEL TODAY **MY GREATEST CHALLENGE**

MOOD TRACKER:

MORNING: EVENING:

I FELT HAPPY WHEN: I FELT EXCITED WHEN: I FELT ENERGIZED WHEN:

Today's Highlights

What I'm Grateful For Today

DATE:

DAILY *Reflection*

HOW I FEEL TODAY MY GREATEST CHALLENGE

MOOD TRACKER:

MORNING: EVENING:

I FELT HAPPY WHEN: I FELT EXCITED WHEN: I FELT ENERGIZED WHEN:

Today's Highlights

What I'm Grateful For Today

DATE:

DAILY *Reflection*

HOW I FEEL TODAY **MY GREATEST CHALLENGE**

MOOD TRACKER:

MORNING: **EVENING:**

I FELT HAPPY WHEN: **I FELT EXCITED WHEN:** **I FELT ENERGIZED WHEN:**

Today's Highlights

What I'm Grateful For Today

DATE:

DAILY Reflection

HOW I FEEL TODAY

MY GREATEST CHALLENGE

MOOD TRACKER:

MORNING:

EVENING:

I FELT HAPPY WHEN:

I FELT EXCITED WHEN:

I FELT ENERGIZED WHEN:

Today's Highlights

What I'm Grateful For Today

DAILY *Reflection*

DATE:

HOW I FEEL TODAY

MY GREATEST CHALLENGE

MOOD TRACKER:

MORNING:

EVENING:

I FELT HAPPY WHEN:

I FELT EXCITED WHEN:

I FELT ENERGIZED WHEN:

Today's Highlights

What I'm Grateful For Today

DATE:

DAILY *Reflection*

HOW I FEEL TODAY **MY GREATEST CHALLENGE**

MOOD TRACKER:

MORNING: EVENING:

I FELT HAPPY WHEN: I FELT EXCITED WHEN: I FELT ENERGIZED WHEN:

Today's Highlights

What I'm Grateful For Today

WEEKLY Assessment

	SLEEP	MOOD	POSITIVES	NEGATIVES
MONDAY				
TUESDAY				
WEDNESDAY				
THURSDAY				
FRIDAY				
SATURADY				
SUNDAY				

MOOD *Chart*

Use the wheel below to document your moods every month.
Use 3 different colors to represent positive, negative or neutral emotions.

☐ **POSITIVE**   ☐ **NEGATIVE**   ☐ **NEUTRAL**

MONTH:

SLEEP *Tracker*

MONTH: _____

Sleep plays a major factor in our ability to cope with anxiety. Keep track of your sleep pattern in order to determine how the amount of rest may be affecting your mental health.

DAY	HOURS SLEPT	QUALITY OF SLEEP	THOUGHTS
1			
2			
3			
4			
5			
6			
7			
8			
9			
10			
11			
12			
13			
14			
15			
16			
17			
18			
19			
20			
21			
22			
23			
24			
25			
26			
27			
28			
29			
30			
31			

DATE:

DAILY *Reflection*

HOW I FEEL TODAY **MY GREATEST CHALLENGE**

MOOD TRACKER:

MORNING: EVENING:

I FELT HAPPY WHEN: I FELT EXCITED WHEN: I FELT ENERGIZED WHEN:

Today's Highlights

What I'm Grateful For Today

DATE:

DAILY *Reflection*

HOW I FEEL TODAY

MY GREATEST CHALLENGE

MOOD TRACKER:

MORNING:

EVENING:

I FELT HAPPY WHEN:

I FELT EXCITED WHEN:

I FELT ENERGIZED WHEN:

Today's Highlights

What I'm Grateful For Today

DATE:

DAILY Reflection

HOW I FEEL TODAY　　　　　　　　　　　　　　　　**MY GREATEST CHALLENGE**

MOOD TRACKER:

MORNING:　　　　　　　　　　　　EVENING:

I FELT HAPPY WHEN:　　　　I FELT EXCITED WHEN:　　　　I FELT ENERGIZED WHEN:

Today's Highlights

What I'm Grateful For Today

DATE:

DAILY Reflection

HOW I FEEL TODAY

MY GREATEST CHALLENGE

MOOD TRACKER:

MORNING:

EVENING:

I FELT HAPPY WHEN:

I FELT EXCITED WHEN:

I FELT ENERGIZED WHEN:

Today's Highlights

What I'm Grateful For Today

DATE:

DAILY *Reflection*

HOW I FEEL TODAY

MY GREATEST CHALLENGE

MOOD TRACKER:

MORNING:

EVENING:

I FELT HAPPY WHEN:

I FELT EXCITED WHEN:

I FELT ENERGIZED WHEN:

Today's Highlights

What I'm Grateful For Today

DATE:

DAILY *Reflection*

HOW I FEEL TODAY **MY GREATEST CHALLENGE**

MOOD TRACKER:

MORNING: **EVENING:**

I FELT HAPPY WHEN: **I FELT EXCITED WHEN:** **I FELT ENERGIZED WHEN:**

Today's Highlights

What I'm Grateful For Today

DATE:

DAILY Reflection

HOW I FEEL TODAY　　　　　　　　　　　　　**MY GREATEST CHALLENGE**

MOOD TRACKER:

MORNING:　　　　　　　　　　**EVENING:**

I FELT HAPPY WHEN:　　　**I FELT EXCITED WHEN:**　　　**I FELT ENERGIZED WHEN:**

Today's Highlights

What I'm Grateful For Today

WEEKLY *Assessment*

	SLEEP	MOOD	POSITIVES	NEGATIVES
MONDAY				
TUESDAY				
WEDNESDAY				
THURSDAY				
FRIDAY				
SATURADY				
SUNDAY				

DATE:

DAILY *Reflection*

HOW I FEEL TODAY **MY GREATEST CHALLENGE**

MOOD TRACKER:

MORNING: EVENING:

I FELT HAPPY WHEN: I FELT EXCITED WHEN: I FELT ENERGIZED WHEN:

Today's Highlights

What I'm Grateful For Today

DATE:

DAILY *Reflection*

HOW I FEEL TODAY MY GREATEST CHALLENGE

MOOD TRACKER:

MORNING: EVENING:

I FELT HAPPY WHEN: I FELT EXCITED WHEN: I FELT ENERGIZED WHEN:

Today's Highlights

What I'm Grateful For Today

DATE:

DAILY *Reflection*

HOW I FEEL TODAY **MY GREATEST CHALLENGE**

MOOD TRACKER:

MORNING: EVENING:

I FELT HAPPY WHEN: I FELT EXCITED WHEN: I FELT ENERGIZED WHEN:

Today's Highlights

What I'm Grateful For Today

DATE:

DAILY *Reflection*

HOW I FEEL TODAY **MY GREATEST CHALLENGE**

MOOD TRACKER:

MORNING: EVENING:

I FELT HAPPY WHEN: **I FELT EXCITED WHEN:** **I FELT ENERGIZED WHEN:**

Today's Highlights

What I'm Grateful For Today

DATE:

DAILY *Reflection*

HOW I FEEL TODAY **MY GREATEST CHALLENGE**

MOOD TRACKER:

MORNING: **EVENING:**

I FELT HAPPY WHEN: **I FELT EXCITED WHEN:** **I FELT ENERGIZED WHEN:**

Today's Highlights

What I'm Grateful For Today

DATE:

DAILY *Reflection*

HOW I FEEL TODAY

MY GREATEST CHALLENGE

MOOD TRACKER:

MORNING:

EVENING:

I FELT HAPPY WHEN:

I FELT EXCITED WHEN:

I FELT ENERGIZED WHEN:

Today's Highlights

What I'm Grateful For Today

DATE:

DAILY Reflection

HOW I FEEL TODAY MY GREATEST CHALLENGE

MOOD TRACKER:

MORNING: EVENING:

I FELT HAPPY WHEN: I FELT EXCITED WHEN: I FELT ENERGIZED WHEN:

Today's Highlights

What I'm Grateful For Today

WEEKLY Assessment

	SLEEP	MOOD	POSITIVES	NEGATIVES
MONDAY				
TUESDAY				
WEDNESDAY				
THURSDAY				
FRIDAY				
SATURADY				
SUNDAY				

DATE:

DAILY *Reflection*

HOW I FEEL TODAY　　　　　　　　　　　　　　　**MY GREATEST CHALLENGE**

MOOD TRACKER:

MORNING:　　　　　　　　　　　　　　EVENING:

I FELT HAPPY WHEN:　　　　I FELT EXCITED WHEN:　　　　I FELT ENERGIZED WHEN:

Today's Highlights

What I'm Grateful For Today

DAILY *Reflection*

DATE:

HOW I FEEL TODAY

MY GREATEST CHALLENGE

MOOD TRACKER:

MORNING:

EVENING:

I FELT HAPPY WHEN:

I FELT EXCITED WHEN:

I FELT ENERGIZED WHEN:

Today's Highlights

What I'm Grateful For Today

DATE:

DAILY *Reflection*

HOW I FEEL TODAY MY GREATEST CHALLENGE

MOOD TRACKER:

MORNING: EVENING:

I FELT HAPPY WHEN: I FELT EXCITED WHEN: I FELT ENERGIZED WHEN:

Today's Highlights

What I'm Grateful For Today

DAILY *Reflection*

DATE:

HOW I FEEL TODAY

MY GREATEST CHALLENGE

MOOD TRACKER:

MORNING:

EVENING:

I FELT HAPPY WHEN:

I FELT EXCITED WHEN:

I FELT ENERGIZED WHEN:

Today's Highlights

What I'm Grateful For Today

DATE:

DAILY *Reflection*

HOW I FEEL TODAY

MY GREATEST CHALLENGE

MOOD TRACKER:

MORNING:

EVENING:

I FELT HAPPY WHEN:

I FELT EXCITED WHEN:

I FELT ENERGIZED WHEN:

Today's Highlights

What I'm Grateful For Today

DATE:

DAILY *Reflection*

HOW I FEEL TODAY **MY GREATEST CHALLENGE**

MOOD TRACKER:

MORNING: EVENING:

I FELT HAPPY WHEN: **I FELT EXCITED WHEN:** **I FELT ENERGIZED WHEN:**

Today's Highlights

What I'm Grateful For Today

DATE:

DAILY Reflection

HOW I FEEL TODAY MY GREATEST CHALLENGE

MOOD TRACKER:

MORNING: EVENING:

I FELT HAPPY WHEN: I FELT EXCITED WHEN: I FELT ENERGIZED WHEN:

Today's Highlights

What I'm Grateful For Today

WEEKLY *Assessment*

	SLEEP	MOOD	POSITIVES	NEGATIVES
MONDAY				
TUESDAY				
WEDNESDAY				
THURSDAY				
FRIDAY				
SATURADY				
SUNDAY				

DATE:

DAILY Reflection

HOW I FEEL TODAY **MY GREATEST CHALLENGE**

MOOD TRACKER:

MORNING: **EVENING:**

I FELT HAPPY WHEN: **I FELT EXCITED WHEN:** **I FELT ENERGIZED WHEN:**

Today's Highlights

What I'm Grateful For Today

DAILY *Reflection*

DATE:

HOW I FEEL TODAY

MY GREATEST CHALLENGE

MOOD TRACKER:

MORNING:

EVENING:

I FELT HAPPY WHEN:

I FELT EXCITED WHEN:

I FELT ENERGIZED WHEN:

Today's Highlights

What I'm Grateful For Today

DATE:

DAILY *Reflection*

HOW I FEEL TODAY **MY GREATEST CHALLENGE**

MOOD TRACKER:

MORNING: EVENING:

I FELT HAPPY WHEN: **I FELT EXCITED WHEN:** **I FELT ENERGIZED WHEN:**

Today's Highlights

What I'm Grateful For Today

DATE:

DAILY *Reflection*

HOW I FEEL TODAY

MY GREATEST CHALLENGE

MOOD TRACKER:

MORNING:

EVENING:

I FELT HAPPY WHEN:

I FELT EXCITED WHEN:

I FELT ENERGIZED WHEN:

Today's Highlights

What I'm Grateful For Today

DATE:

DAILY *Reflection*

HOW I FEEL TODAY **MY GREATEST CHALLENGE**

MOOD TRACKER:

MORNING: EVENING:

I FELT HAPPY WHEN: I FELT EXCITED WHEN: I FELT ENERGIZED WHEN:

Today's Highlights

What I'm Grateful For Today

DATE:

DAILY Reflection

HOW I FEEL TODAY **MY GREATEST CHALLENGE**

MOOD TRACKER:

MORNING: **EVENING:**

I FELT HAPPY WHEN: **I FELT EXCITED WHEN:** **I FELT ENERGIZED WHEN:**

Today's Highlights

What I'm Grateful For Today

DATE:

DAILY *Reflection*

HOW I FEEL TODAY **MY GREATEST CHALLENGE**

MOOD TRACKER:

MORNING: **EVENING:**

I FELT HAPPY WHEN: **I FELT EXCITED WHEN:** **I FELT ENERGIZED WHEN:**

Today's Highlights

What I'm Grateful For Today

WEEKLY Assessment

	SLEEP	MOOD	POSITIVES	NEGATIVES
MONDAY				
TUESDAY				
WEDNESDAY				
THURSDAY				
FRIDAY				
SATURADY				
SUNDAY				

Printed in Great Britain
by Amazon